KIMBERLY DAVIS

Alchemies of Loss
(poems)

Dear Laura,
May this collection
offer some comfort.
Much love,
Marita + Howie

Featuring "Alchemy,"
Winner of the 2009-2010 James Wright Poetry Award

Second Edition 2013

ISBN-10: 0983481016
EAN-13: 9780983481010

Bare Cove Press
P.O. Box 699
Hingham, MA 02043

ACKNOWLEDGMENTS

The author wishes to thank Frank Bidart for his extraordinary teaching, and for his patience. Thanks also to Alan Shapiro and Barry Goldensohn for small edits that made a huge difference, and to Peg and Bob Boyers for providing an invaluable writing community at the New York State Summer Writers Institute at Skidmore College.

The author also wishes to thank the editors of the literary journals where some of these poems have appeared, and the judges and organizers of the contests where two of these poems have received recognition:

"Thumbprint on Estate Papers" originally appeared in briefer version in *The Iowa Review*, Vol. 29, No. 3. In its current form, this poem won First Prize in Poetry and the Benefactor's Prize at the 2007 Whidbey Island Writers Conference. Thanks to the conference organizers and to the judges, who gave the author the courage to persevere.

"Prayerstone" and "King Alfreds, First Light" appeared in *Nimrod International Literary Journal*, Vol. 49, No. 2 ("The Healing Arts," Spring/Summer 2006).

"Tree" and "Visions" appeared in *Cairn*, Nos. 42 (2007) and 45 (2010), respectively.

"Grief Redecorated Your House" appeared in *The Briar Cliff Review*, Vol. 20 (2008).

"Alchemy" appeared in *Mid-American Review* Vol. XXX, Nos. 1 and 2, and was the winner of the 2009–2010 James Wright Poetry Award sponsored by that magazine. Special thanks to contest judge Carl Dennis, whose own work the author greatly admires.

Cover

Cover photograph of the "Weeping Angel" of Hingham used by
permission of John Hooper Dean (jack@ourweepingangel.org).

Donations to the alternative healing fund at the Our Weeping Angel
Foundation may be made online at www.ourweepingangel.org.

In memory of Janet Davis (1933–1994)

CONTENTS

Alchemies of Loss

Four AM

and I find myself again
in the church

of the dark hours, coffee
and preternatural awareness

like a cat's eye-shine. Everything

is still,
so still and quiet, except for

steam and scent escaping
the glass carafe. The blackness all around,

sentient, permeable—like a membrane
I could plunge my hand through

and bring back
a red rose, a handful of dirt. Above the table,

a lamp. Out of porous night
I have carved

this small
room of light.

Away

The moon holds her head
in her blue hands—

How could you be so foolish?

She is referring to the casual
remark I made to the wrong person.

Her cheek rolls through wisps
of white clouds, chiding me, but then
forbearing. She knows, like her,

I'm better at reflection,
a bit dim in the moment.

My mood will lift
if I follow her out

across stubbled fields
where we can hide

in the branches of bare trees
and no one needs

say anything

Tree

It seems now
that I have never believed
in the unyielding nature
of physical objects. How strange
that you could stretch out
on the floor, for example,
and not fall through,
or lean against a wall
for hours, going nowhere.
How easily the mind tips sideways
and plunges into
what's hidden back there—
the colonies of military mice,
the secret crawlspaces.
I imagine the centers of trees
as hollow, luminous chambers
within which dust motes swirl,
glinting in moonlight.
How, then, could one so suddenly
have stopped his car?
Some things the mind simply refuses.
But perhaps he did break through
to unite with
the sparkling dust,
the circling breeze
lifting him up, up.

Apples, Angels

I realized today
it was fourteen years
since I last saw you

and yet you are
as real to me now

and nearly as close
your embracing presence

I walked
to the graveyard

though not the one where
you are buried in upstate New York—
I thought you'd enjoy

the weeping angel
behind the church
her girlish shoulders
bent over the headstone
of someone named Hooper
her wings adroop.

Then we went
to the little grocery downtown
where we discussed
whether to wash the pesticides
from the glowing Washington apples
or buy the pathetic organic ones
from Chile. You worried

about such things.
You still do.

Alchemy

I would like to have a catalog of what
each day is worth, weighed in

I don't know, the most

interesting stones you
could find on a beach, or colored glass

tortured luminous by a million
grains of sand—the effects

of this wearing down
upon my spirit I am

only just beginning
to fathom. After my mother's death

I wondered what indignity
would be next, and how far

it would take me
along this path

which starts to brighten
as more is stripped away.

I see now
what comes of loss

                    and I
am beginning to hold to it

the way the alchemist clings
to a clot of iron

summoning gold.

Stone Angels

An hour ago, it began
to rain, the sound

outside like sand
through an hourglass. Now

it is growing darker or
the lamp stronger—hard to say,

almost as if the room
were pulling to the glow. I was

supposed to be somewhere,
but two glasses of wine
solved that. I'm no good

when it's late—the evenings
how sad they become

filled with people
I used to love, gone now,

who want me to remember
their soft forms, backlit, the way

they laughed out loud
at the things you said. Well, at least

they are here, if
always the same, always

the same

Girl in the Woods

Left alone
for the evening—I was twelve
and we lived far back
half a mile from the nearest
neighbor by a forest path. It was fall
and raining, the soaked
boughs heavy on the roof. Perhaps
it was a limb
landing with a thump
that sent me bolting from the house, my
long hair and thin coat flying.

Did I really believe
someone was on the roof? Did I see
a face in the window? For that is
what I told the kind neighbor lady
when she answered the door. I think I
must have lied.
I was alone in an empty house.
I got scared.
I ran.

But perhaps I did see a ghost or
a premonition of one—
A few months later my
father would be gone his
car having strayed from the road
on just such a night—tires
skidding on sodden leaves—

I'm a grown woman now, and safe
and dry in my own home. I gaze
past rain-drizzled windows. A young girl
is out there in the forest, her eyes
wide with terror, her hair drenched. She is
making her way towards me even now.
I long to invite her in, and bring her tea
and a towel for her hair, and tell her
it's all right, but I know
she will never arrive.

The path through the woods
is treacherous. Her feet slip—ankles scuff
on stones and roots. She grasps
dripping branches for balance, her eyes
black to the night like a wild creature. Far ahead
she spies a swirl of brilliance
in the steamy air—

*the porch light
she will never reach*

No, she is not lost,
but it is late, and the dark
wilderness of the psyche,
boundless.

Thumbprint on Estate Papers

A cola-brown whorl I had to taste
on what are now your estate papers—
yes, you were eating chocolate

on a hot day. How like you,
who spent the money Dad left
on what's-his-name and all those gowns

still ballroom dancing in my closet,
chiffon and feathers swinging on hangers
in the dark each time I shut the door.

As you were dying, you reverted
to the maddening innocence of a child,
asked what you'd done to deserve such pain.

"I've been a good girl," you cried.
You weren't. Careless and charming
as your own mother, who abandoned you,

left you to trail behind your grandfather—
the grizzled lineman for the power company.
Every summer he shaved the lower forty

with a rusty tractor he let you drive.
At your funeral the aunts told how
you once left it rolling to chase a moth,

but I picture you riding high,
rattling and shaking atop baler and rake,
clanking over the scraggy ground—

You double clutch with bare dirty feet,
your toes spreading to reach the pedals,
jouncing on your patched jeans seat.

At the end of the pass I see you spin
the thin iron wheel with the cool delight
of a sportscar driver, half out of control,

swerving around, and then reeling true
to a plan so absurdly larger than you—
a perfect thumbprint from three miles up.

King Alfreds, First Light

The King Alfred daffodils lean into the light.
Pink! says the light, and *Orange!*
The sunlight opens like a speaker, with jokes.
The daffodils tolerate him. In an hour
He will shine them an earnest yellow.
And so they lean—how far I never noticed,
Like fishing poles with yellow lures
Or cups on sticks dipping for yellow in a well,
Like bugles blowing after a yellow note.

Blowing for the forsythia, the crocus.
Early spring lets in a spill of blue, a dab of white,
Squills, snowdrops—but only as counterpoint,
Only to invent a purer yellow.
Yellow that aches with its lack of irony.
Yellow that is more a belief in color
Than the color itself, fall's dying
Muted golds purified and resurrected.
What endures after the winter is yellow.

Why can't my daffodils be more like the tulips?
Late risers!—Agnostics standing straight up,
Pleased with any color so long as it can go to a party,
Lipstick reds and cocktail-bar purples, tulips in green
Throats, tulips sporting frilly petals,
We're talking *tulips*.
People say the daffodils are happy. They're wrong.
Just look at how they crane their yellow selves,
Straining on arched green stems,
Searching, wounded, soulful—
Kings of trying to understand.

Prayerstone

When she was ten, and her father lay
pallid and curled in a bed
that buckled at the waist and knees,
she went to her room and,
hugging herself, set her will
against his death like two hands
braced on the boulder they'd seen
near Lake Placid. Kidney-shaped,
the great rock stood
in an open field, lichens slowly
inscribing blue-green and mustard
circles on its face and shoulders.
"An erratic," they said, explaining
nothing. Determined to budge it—
she was determined, if only an inch.
An inch was all her father required
to free his life from the musty vault
under that granite slab,
a fissure she would open
with the fervency of her mind.
No mere prayer was this.

After he died she felt
not that she had been too weak,
but that her resolve had faltered,
betrayed by thoughts
which could already imagine him gone.
How they tugged at her hands
like little children
peeling back her fingers
one by one. Then she remembered,
water had carried that stone,
lifted it and carried it
all the way from Quebec
nestled in the body
of a frozen sea:
A miraculous voyage.

Grief Redecorated Your House

This I will say for grief. It made everything new.
Were you tired of your clothing? Wished for
a new suit or blouse? How
can you wear a new blouse
in the presence of grief?
A new *blue* blouse.
How could you? How
could you even care
what color? Were you bored
with your furniture, of living
with the same sofa year after year. Grief
redecorated your house
with outrage. Nothing
was the same, not the paint
on the walls, not the walls themselves,
not the atoms holding up the walls
in all that empty space.

Upon Hearing of the Death of Paul Barclay

The objects in this room, they have
completely given up on me—

the lamp, tossing its yellow
disks without regard

the television, proclaiming
what's coming up next

as if you could not
be harmed, could not feel

the merciless demand to
carry on
in the usual way. If I could,

I would plug in only
the black cord to the damaged

clock that refuses to move. (That clock is on my side.)

If only an act of will
were all that was required

to halt the progress of
what is already gone—

you, Paul,
older cousin when I was eight, the beauty
of your long wrists and tangled hair,

the way you barely noticed me.

After Sunset, Returning from the Hospital

Darkened sparrows bore holes
in a gaping sky—

transparent vessel
of emerging stars. The sound

of nothing, like a grand eraser
sweeping a pale chalk of clouds

from a lucent moon. Behind the visible,
spectral wings where

twin eternities meet
and we see in an instant

birth and destruction are
the same thing
mirrored. Oh, what shall I do

with the size of it all
with the scale. How can I open

the solid door of the car, traverse the distance to
the ever-diminishing house. This

awful feeling—if only I

could hold it down, quivering,
but it will not keep still—

flies up, flapping.

Duration

And so your life seems to have
collapsed like a paper fan—each day

a child is being run down by a car
in the past. Someone's

hair is catching fire
once,

but what year?—You told a friend
your mother had died four years ago.

It was fourteen years. And still she is

writhing in a morphine haze, one
leg missing, and you are

standing at the nurses station, begging for
help, where you will always be standing.

At that desk. In that hall. Fending off
the fluid that would not

stop weeping from that unimaginable
stump, the rack

it caused in your mind. You have tried
distraction, gratitude, shaking your head

very hard—if only you
could go far enough away

but these things
they are always coming near

A Cricket Holds Back the Dawn

Here at the threshold of
what comes next, let

the last things

that will occur
occur. Outside the dark window

a song commences

that will soon end—morning arriving
with inexorable grace, as it does

every morning. The window briefly encloses

space invisible, ungraspable, which the light
will convert to trees,

clouds, a measurable sky—and yet,

as the cricket told (black, cheerful, insane)—
that moment, framed,

has always existed, always will exist

in the appalling place where
time does not run only

in one direction, eternal location

where the lost souls reside
in the stale grandeur of annihilation. Hear the call-note

of the ceaseless torrent, played by
the fiddler

for the extinguishing present

Visions

A tree holds out upon its leaves
shivering globes of rain

the sun passes behind a cloud | the light dims

how strange is
                perception

especially now
for my mother-in-law—she has been seeing
at the foot of her bed

people, most of whom
happen to be small

she gazes without alarm at this new world
she does not frighten me

when I enter her sterile
populous room

confusion glances across
her expression—I might be

One of Them. Then I bend to

kiss my husband
who is seated nearby

and you can see her thinking

       if she's real | what is real

Early Morning

Blankets around our feet
in pre-dawn stillness

our bellies exposed

the little dog snoring
on the pillow

no current of air
no stir

to rouse the skin, only

probable dust
so fine

I cannot see
cannot feel or hear

its careful fingers upon us, its
mortal whisper
                come vulnerable flesh ...

Out the windows a white
veil lifts off birches. Soon

a breeze will wake
the heartshaped leaves, but for now
they sleep

lightly, uncovered
like us.

Waiting for the Results

each time
is like sitting in the antechamber
to eternity. So it was for my mother

and now, me
at the age she started to get
too skinny.

If I take a walk without the cell phone
I seem to have been granted a reprieve

for as long as my legs
can keep moving. There is a sense of such
fettered happiness

out in that air (that absurd June air).

When I crest the hill by the Old Ship Church
built of timbers from the early sixteen hundreds

I feel sorry for the people who huddle in there
each Sunday, yet generous
towards them. They are my people

and I want to bring them out
and show them

this street
these trees, this sky

Perennial

Late August. The tall phlox
keeled over in a sudden downpour—
puffy white blooms with soft pink eyes,
they put me in mind of the elderly lady
who lived next door at the old house.
Her husband had passed away
at ninety, and she was staying active
dividing her few perennials. She hefted
green shoots across her picket fence
in a galvanized bucket, dowager's
wings rising on her shoulders.
She was giving things away—
not just flowers—a brass candle snuffer
for my little boy, her car
to her granddaughter, the nurse. Now we
have moved, and she endures
inside her white Cape house
growing paler and more elegantly dressed
each time we visit—beige cardigan
of uncombed wool, iridescent
freshwater pearls. This summer we
haven't found the time. Busy. Perhaps
we are afraid—

that we will knock and knock,
there is no answer—
Suddenly my son is pointing
to the second floor dormer,
up-flung sash, curtain blown out
and trailing like a scarf.
No, higher—see the fledgling geese
beating south on new pinions,
going where they have never been,
where they cannot resist going.

Country Church
Salisbury Center, NY

Plainest of all bright forms
on a dark ground

white anvil

where I sat with her body
retching tears that I no longer

remember—stark compass to
something called

hereafter | place

of light shining
from the next valley, or elsewhere—

pearl suspended in mountain shadow

—END—

ABOUT THE AUTHOR

Kimberly Davis is a poet and writer who grew up with roots deep in the Adirondack foothills of upstate New York. She received her undergraduate degree from Brown University and her MFA in creative writing from Emerson College. Her work has appeared in many fine literary journals. She now lives in Hingham, Massachusetts, with her husband Steve and son Daniel.

Alchemies of Loss began as Davis's response to the loss of her mother, Janet Davis, to cancer in 1994. Over the years, this project has grown into the group of twenty poems that comprise the current chapbook.

Davis is also the author of the memoir *Teaching the Dog to Think*, about her crash introduction to the sport of dog agility. For more information about author Kimberly Davis, please visit her website at http://kimberlysdavis.com.

34634480R00029

Made in the USA
Charleston, SC
14 October 2014